TECHNOLOGY IN LANGUAGE LEAR
(*Series editor* Brian Hill)

Making the most of video

Brian Hill

Illustrations by Pieter Sluis

C*i*LT

First published 1989
© 1989 Centre for Information on Language Teaching and Research
ISBN 0 948003 18 9

Cover design by Pieter Sluis
Printed in Great Britain by C.M.D. Limited

Published by Centre for Information on Language Teaching and Research, Regent's College, Inner Circle, London NW1 4NS

All rights reserved. No part of the publication may be reproduced, stored in a retrieval system, or transmitted in any form or by any means, electronic, mechanical, photocopying, recording, or otherwise, without the prior permission of the Copyright owner.

Contents

	Page
CHAPTER ONE	1
CHAPTER TWO	8
CHAPTER THREE	19
CHAPTER FOUR	31
CHAPTER FIVE	42
GLOSSARY	49

CHAPTER ONE

Introduction

Making the most of video is intended as a practical guide to help language teachers, whether of English or foreign languages, exploit the potential of television. Its main focus is on the establishment of a 'portfolio of good practice' with concrete ideas for using the medium, illustrated with examples from current programmes. Also included is a chapter to set the scene, some thoughts on organisational alternatives and a discussion of technical considerations both as a basis for purchasing decisions and to get the most out of the equipment.

In the past, target audiences for programmes were specifically defined. Both BBC and ITV, for instance, often labelled their language series as being for particular school age groups or 'for adults'; the implication being that the material would only be suitable for those belonging to these groups. Recently, experience has led to a dismantling of these barriers. It has been realised that 'continuing education' programmes can just as easily be used in schools, and vice versa. Adaptation is made easier since all series are accompanied by transcripts or teacher's notes which help in selecting different exploitation techniques to suit the nature of the class. Similarly, the barriers between the world of English as a Foreign Language and foreign language teaching in Britain have largely disappeared and it has become clear that ideas for classroom activities are likely to be equally valid whatever the language.

In *Making the most of video*, therefore, the reader will find examples of exercises which are primarily in English and French. The ideas behind the activities, however, are usually applicable to any language. In the same vein, an example might be drawn from a programme designated as being 'for adults', but there are very few ideas and techniques which cannot be exploited across the whole spectrum of language teaching whether for younger or for older learners.

These last few years have been exciting ones for language teachers. We have experienced or, in many cases, provoked a linguistic revolution. The theoretical advantages of communicative teaching have been widely accepted. We want, and indeed we are expected, to produce students/pupils who can comprehend accurately and speak with confidence; pupils who can also understand the cultural, social, economic and political backgrounds of the countries whose language they are studying. Language training is increasingly seen as a practical skill that leads to contact with foreigners at a variety of different levels. Most members of the profession and our 'clients' have welcomed this significant change of emphasis. The linguistic revolution has been prompted, or at least fuelled, by pressure from outside. The European Community, the world's largest grouping of people, is a reality. Trade across language frontiers has increased dramatically and this will continue. More and more people can expect to spend a proportion of their working lives abroad, or at least, in close contact with foreign countries. Travel is getting easier; the Tunnel, more and cheaper flights, better trains, all contribute to the relative ease with which borders can be crossed. Most schools and colleges have partnership arrangements promoting visits, exchanges and informal contacts. Books, films, journals and newspapers, radio and television programmes are read, heard or seen as a matter of course across national frontiers.

So, the times have never been more propitious for advocates of language teaching and yet this happy situation brings with it a difficult and unique set of problems. We know what is expected, we are broadly in sympathy with the demands made on us (indeed, we have played as a profession no small role in creating these demands), but how do we satisfy the expectations? Are we in danger of being hoist with our own enthusiastic petard?

The fact is that in many ways it is more difficult to deliver communicative goods than when we based our teaching on structuralist objectives. So, we need to develop new approaches, new strategies, new materials, new equipment. It is difficult to see how the fruits of the linguistic revolution can be realised without the judicious application of educational technology. And few of our pedagogic weapons are as valuable in this context as video.

The first point to make very firmly in any consideration of what video offers is that the video recorder cannot and does not replace the teacher. Many managers, thinking primarily of their costs, have been tempted to see an investment in educational technology, including video, as a way of saving in the long term on staff costs. If anything, the effective employment of video within an institution is likely to demand more, rather than less time. In effect, video modifies the teacher's role so that s/he becomes more of a facilitator, a manager, adapting video source material to the needs of individual classes and students. Rarely should learners, particularly beginners and lower intermediate, be exposed to more than two or three minutes at a time. Many videophiles regard twenty seconds as enough to work on. This necessitates the active involvement of the teacher. At an average of 120 words per minute, three minutes of television already confronts the learner with a challenging body of lexis to comprehend and process. In fact, the biggest disappointments in using video have occurred when teachers have been over-ambitious. Television (and of course sound only material) can be much more difficult to comprehend than we realise. It is salutary for every language teacher to try to learn a new language every six or seven years. I learnt more about teaching from attending an evening course in Modern Greek than from any number of pedagogic seminars. We tend to forget what a struggle it is to become fluent in a language. If the tasks we pose, the activities we create or the basic materials we use are too difficult, we create frustration, and learners quickly lose that crucial element of confidence. As a general rule, it is **much better to choose a short excerpt and to work on it thoroughly than to attempt a long, difficult excerpt and to skim over it.**

In this context, the **three-phase approach** has often proved the most effective.

In **Phase one**, just play the video sequence with or without pre-viewing activities to orientate students to what is to come. It is important to stress that you do not expect students to understand every word. Often when using authentic material you will come across a number of words and phrases you do not want learners to spend time on at all.

Phase two is where the detailed teaching and practice takes place. You may, before playing the sequence a second time, wish to signpost some of the vocabulary. It is not advisable, however, to introduce too many words or phrases out of context. The basis of Phase two is 'exploded viewing' where you pause the video frequently to focus attention on specific vocabulary and to initiate teaching and learning activities. Detailed suggestions for what to do are given in Chapters 2-4.

Phase three is for general reinforcement of the work of Phase two. Here you play the sequence again without a pause or, if the material has been fairly challenging and there has been a lot to learn, use 'silent exploded viewing'. For this you pause the video at appropriate points, but say nothing. It just provides an opportunity for the sense of the words to 'sink in' and to enable students to process what is being said.

Why use video?

So much for general thoughts on using video. It seemed important to put them up front to emphasise the crucial nature of the teacher's role. But there are several more specific and tangible reasons as to why video should be a part of every teacher's armoury.

- Television is inherently an attractive and compelling medium that has great potential for motivating learners. No teacher alone can provide the variety of situations, of voices, of accents, of themes, of presentation techniques that are already available in video and which will be increasingly available in the future. A teacher standing before the class day after day, week after week, year after year, needs every support if s/he is not to be drained of initiative, the ability to create dramatic impacts and to successfully manage the complex learning patterns of different students. Television can help the teacher provide the stimulus for motivating and introducing effective learning experience.

- Increasingly, we are wanting to base our teaching on 'exemplars' of 'real' situations. Foreign streets, cafés, railway stations, playing fields, offices and houses are the context for language exploitation. Television can come close to capturing the flavour of reality in these situations giving learners, albeit vicariously, the feeling of participating in, or at least observing, what is actually happening.

- Authentic language is now both the starting point and a prime goal of many language courses. There is no better medium than television for presenting learners with the linguistic material for them to absorb and manipulate as part of the complex and at times tortuous process of acquiring proficiency in a foreign language.

- An important ingredient in presenting real situations and in motivating learners is topicality. The dead-hand of moribund course material has proved a disincentive to many language learners over the years. How much better to have in the classroom material that reflects what is currently happening in the world outside. The possibility of exploiting the students' current interests in sporting events, major news stories, causes for concern or even the weather can best be realised by the introduction of television. A later book in this series on authentic television will look in detail at how to capture and exploit the massive bank of TV material available to us, so it suffices to stress here that the capability to show satellite television or, at least, video tapes sent from abroad provides a particularly important resource we should not ignore.

- In the majority of actual communicative exchanges, participants have the advantage of a range of visual clues integrated implicitly or explicitly with what is being said. Books, sound tapes and computer programs cannot provide this, so, inevitably, lessons developed from these sources are saddled with an inherent artificiality. Television can uniquely provide the range of paralinguistic clues - facial expressions, body movements, visual references - that are so useful for basic comprehension and accurate understanding.

- Increasingly we want to make the language learning experience relevant, and a key ingredient of relevance is weaving the language into an identifiable cultural and social fabric. The visual character of a country - its architecture, its vehicles, its decorations, its customs, its dress, its climate - can be rapidly and effectively conveyed via television. Insights into what makes people tick and the context within which they lead their lives can be attractively presented. Learners, therefore, are able to build up experience of the foreign country, giving them an invaluable, if sometimes intangible context for the language they are studying.

- A major advantage of television is its adaptability; it is capable of flexible exploitation in a wide variety of situations. The same programme can be used to advantage with beginners, intermediate or advanced students for developing listening, speaking or writing skills. A news bulletin, for instance, can provide plenty of meat for advanced learners to study register, to enhance their vocabulary, to do transcription, translation, summary work, etc. At the other end of the spectrum, the same bulletin can be used with virtual beginners for activities such as sequencing, spotting anything which indicates they are in the foreign country, for noting any words at all they understand. A key point to make, well illustrated by this example, is that **the teacher's role is crucial**. It is the teacher who has to take the decision as to how a programme is to be used; there is nothing inherent in the material itself which prevents use for a variety of purposes. Following the same point, it is the teacher who is primarily responsible for the success of the exploitation, not the producers. A programme which is **good** in television terms can be ruined; though conversely and more positively, material that is at first sight **bad** television can be used to advantage, if the correct activities are selected.

● A final advantage of television which is not directly connected with the classroom, but which is nevertheless important, is that television can help develop the teacher's own skill. By regularly viewing authentic television, the teacher could keep 'up to date' with what's happening and ensure that his/her linguistic skills are challenged. Introducing television into the curriculum could provoke a review of linguistic and pedagogic goals, which leads to more relevant and more interesting classroom activities.

Some problems in using video

Whilst most videophiles are enthusiastic and positive about the introduction of television and recognise the advantages outlined above, it is important to remain sanguine and to consider, too, some of the problems associated with the use of video. Since this is a book which is primarily about encouraging and stimulating the use of video, the disadvantages are not presented in a negative light, as some sort of balance to *What video can do*, but rather in the belief that these problems should be defined in order that they can be avoided, or overcome.

● A major reason for disillusionment is technical breakdown. There is obviously no magic solution to this, but it is worth noting that the vast majority of faults reported by teachers are related to minor problems that could/should be cleared up by us. Cables sometimes come loose; the wrong switch for selecting video or television on the receiver is pressed; the wrong channel is chosen on the television or the channel just needs to be re-tuned; 'little fingers' have changed the tracking or mode settings on the video; the video heads get dirty; the television set is not correctly adjusted for colour, contrast or tone. (Technical definitions are considered in more detail in the Glossary) It is, therefore, worth getting yourself thoroughly familiar with the equipment using either the manual or the help of a technician. An hour spent with new equipment just experimenting by yourself with the settings and what happens when the various knobs, buttons and switches are pressed is time well-invested. You soon learn to recognise the most common faults and how to remedy them, thus avoiding many irritating frustrations.

● Following on from this, it is worth making sure that you are getting the optimum picture and sound from the combination of tape, video and television set. It is surprising how often a minor adjustment can make a significant improvement in presentation and, therefore, effectiveness. Don't have the screen facing a window and do position it so that it can be seen from all points in the room. Check for optimum colour and contrast each time you use the set with a different video. Make sure the tracking control on the video is correct for the particular tape you're using. Ensure that you have rapid access to a head-cleaning tape. Try, if possible, to route the sound through an external loud-speaker or, preferably, a sound amplifier. This can dramatically increase the quality of the sound and it can enable you to make adjustments to get the most out of each tape. (Most television sets have the same sound reproduction system as the ones used for domestic televisions in the lounge at home so they are not always adequate for classroom use). Try, if possible, to create an acoustically 'friendly' environment with carpets, curtains and a degree of sound-proofing.

● Group viewing and listening can be difficult. The 'traditional' classroom lay-out is not always suitable, particularly for the generation of inter-active communication within the group. If it is practical, try to group students around the set and get them as close to the sound source as possible. Some teachers, incidentally, play the sound through the language laboratory system. Although this is obviously not ideal for inter-personal oral work, it can improve concentration and develop listening skills as well as leading to individual oral work using the laboratory's recording facilities.

● A feature of the medium itself which can be a disadvantage, particularly vis à vis text-based presentation, is the ephemerality of the television signal. It is rather like a fire-work display, which is full of colour and which makes compulsive viewing but which leaves nothing tangible behind. The key to overcoming this ephemerality lies with the teacher and the activities created to build on and reinforce the viewing experience. Chapters 2-4 describe in detail ways of doing this.

● Television broadcasts are more usually associated with entertainment, and individuals often come to classroom television with passive soporific viewing habits firmly established. Again, it is up to the teacher to make sure that the interface between the screen and the viewer is re-aligned to create more active involvement. Sharing the aims and objectives of what you are trying to do with a particular activity, together with a confident, professional classroom presentation/performance, is often sufficient to secure this attitudinal change.

● Broadcasts have to appeal to a mass audience and this means that a particular programme is unlikely to be exactly right in terms of level, content and style for the group you are teaching. *Follow me*, for instance, the most successful series yet produced, was conceived to be of use to a wide range of learners from businessmen in West Germany to schoolchildren in Thailand, from adults learning around the communal television set in Chinese villages to Scandinavians enjoying the sophisticated facilities of media centres. The role of the teacher, therefore, in taking the 'raw' material and adapting it to the needs of different groups is paramount. The nature of pre- and post-viewing activities and the way in which these activities are presented to the learner will determine the appropriateness of particular programmes, more than the content and style of the programme itself.

● There is an inherent paradox which arises from the nature of the medium. Researchers into the educational use of television have frequently concluded that 'good' television **can** produce 'bad' learning material. The impact of the many techniques available to producers is sometimes so strong that the 'message' is obscured. Viewers are so hypnotised by the succession of visual images that the essence of the learning point is lost. This is not, of course, an argument for 'bad' television, nor for the creation of second-class programmes for educational use; it is the definition of a feature of which the teacher should be aware and which s/he should be able to turn to advantage. There are, perhaps, particular dangers for language teaching/learning programmes. Frequently, we are using television as a basis for developing listening or speaking skills and not, as in many other areas, for presenting information. For us, the sound-track is at least as important as the visuals and it is, therefore, important that we devise activities which direct attention to what is being said. We can indeed make use of motivating and informative visuals, but there will be many occasions when the primary objective of using video will be to develop active listening. The key to re-directing students' attention is often to adopt a sort of Brechtian *Epic Television* technique where the pause button is used to arrest the impact of the visual flow to make students react to what is being said.

● Information and publicity is often difficult to come by. Sources of materials are listed in the Glossary and it is well worth making sure that you are aware of what is available.

● Finally, copyright laws can seem frustratingly restrictive to the effective use of video. Basically, the law prevents the copying or reproduction of video material. Recording off-air is usually allowed, however, provided the programmes recorded are in an educational slot, and tapes are destroyed after a period of time. In the UK this is three years for schools broadcasts and one year for programmes transmitted in the continuing education slots. Most educational authorities now take a firm line on this to stay on the right side of the law, but many programmes are repeated, thus effectively extending the legal life of any tapes recorded. Publishers, too, are usually sympathetic to requests for permission to copy tapes from one standard to another and, sometimes, to requests to allow copying to facilitate use of a video within schools and colleges. [*At the time of writing revision of the copyright laws for educational use is being considered and the above information may change.*]

CHAPTER TWO

Using video to develop listening skills

In this book the skills of listening, speaking and writing are being treated separately. This is not because they can in practice be isolated - they are clearly inter-dependent - but rather in the belief that we should be very careful that we give due prominence in our curricula to developing effective and accurate listening. The key to good oral performance lies as much in developing aural acuity as in speaking practice.

Too often, video activities are created where the output or the success are judged purely on oral performance, with successful listening not being accorded specific and explicit recognition. Many teachers, when asked at the end of a lesson which focused primarily on getting learners to speak what they had been intending, indicated that a main objective of the session was to develop listening skills.

There are a number of reasons why explicit listening activities should be given prominence in curricula and why confusion of listening and speaking objectives should be avoided.

- Learners can process far more vocabulary, far more language if they are not being asked for an oral response. *I can understand, but I can't speak* is a comment frequently heard from learners. We must make sure that we recognise this fact and use it to our advantage, allowing students to build on what they perceive they can do easily and naturally. The possession of a secure base of passive understanding is an excellent starting point for later oral work. There is, then, a strong argument for confronting learners, particularly at the beginning of their language learning careers, with activities which are deliberately designed to promote gist understanding and active listening without the 'intrusion' of oral production. If this is done, the basic foundations of the language linked to the effective mastery of receptive skills can be securely laid, far more vocabulary can be mastered and wider experience of the language gained.

- Linked to this is the key word **confidence**. Alongside motivation, the development of confidence is a crucial pre-requisite of language learning. Working on sounds coming from a loud-speaker in rooms that are often not acoustically ideal, learners have more difficulties than we often realise. We must be cautious when using video that we don't demand the performance of tasks which are too difficult. There is strong evidence that adult learners who drop out from courses do so for reasons that can be summarised as: *I was made to say too much, too soon; I couldn't do it and I felt stupid.* There is then a need to ensure that we deliberately build up rather than destroy confidence and, for many learners, this translates into giving them opportunities for feeling they have been successful in tackling something in which that success was not judged purely in terms of their oral production.

- We often forget just how difficult it is even to answer a question in class, particularly one based on a video programme. An unfortunately typical use of television is for the teacher to play through a substantial chunk of a programme and then simply to ask questions on it. Armed with a transcript and being familiar with the material, teachers do not always empathise with the learners' problems. And yet a complex and demanding process is necessary to enable a successful answer to be given to even a simple question:

- the student has to recognise the language items in the source material;
- the student has to comprehend the source material;
- what s/he has comprehended needs to be held in the short-term memory;
- the student then has to comprehend the teacher's question and search for the required information;
- this information has to be expressed immediately using a correct accent, correct intonation, correct grammar, correct vocabulary often in front of peers with whom the student does not wish to lose face.

There are, as will be suggested, many activities that are valid and worth-while which use video in more fruitful ways than the question-answer mode.

● In highlighting the need to develop listening skills in their own right, we should be aware that in the 'real' world we spend more time on activities using receptive skills than active oral or written skills. There is, in this context, evidence to suggest that there are close links between the acquisition of listening and reading skills. In a survey of learners using BBC language courses (*Foreign Languages by Radio and Television*), many learners commented that they felt their reading skills had improved even though these had not been explicitly practised in the series.

● Before moving on to suggest how to use video effectively, we should note the difference between gist comprehension and 'active listening' or 'listening to learn'. In the world outside language learning, our listening almost invariably involves listening for information. **What** is being said is more important than **how** it is being expressed. Operating in our native language, we are rarely called upon to consider the way in which language is delivered; we focus more naturally on the content. For language learning purposes, however, we need to focus more explicitly on the vehicle, the form of the language, than on the message being conveyed. This observation underlines the need to create listening activities that actively involve the learner in becoming aware of the 'how' as being at least as important as the 'what'.

It is important, therefore, to create a 'taxonomy' of video uses which can be applied according to the professional judgment of the teacher to meet the needs of different classes. The following suggestions for stimulating listening practice contain many examples which are familiar in text-based activities, but which often require a different methodological approach to adapt them successfully to video. They rely primarily on non-verbal outputs by the students, thus focusing principally on the development of active listening. They are designed to promote mental effort, an essential ingredient of successful learning.

In the following suggestions for use, activities to develop recognition precede those which reinforce the meaning of words and phrases. The first suggestions are primarily for use at beginners' level with the difficulty gradually being increased. Whilst the activities themselves can obviously be adapted for any language, most exemplars are given in English.

★ Hunting or spotting activities

The aim here is to get words or phrases to stick in learners' minds and to give them a purpose for listening, even if they don't understand everything.
It is linked to the pre-comprehension stage of **recognition**.

- In its simplest form this type of activity just requires learners to indicate yes/no to whether they heard a particular word or phrase.
- It can also be tackled as a sort of word soup or word/phrase bingo where learners are given a list of, say, twelve phrases, seven of which appear in a sequence, five of which do not. The task is then to tick off those they hear.

Put a ✓.... by those phrases you hear.

in the station	☐
at 9 o'clock	☐
holding a newspaper	☐
a red jacket	☐
	☐

★ Word frequency grids

This is another way of focusing attention on recognising key vocabulary. Here, learners are asked to put a ✓.... every time they hear a word or phrase.

	1	2	3	4	5	6
Follow me						
Thank you						
Over here						
Can you?						

★ Who said what?

Still aiming to build up aural acuity and recognition skills, this activity is best introduced to students during the second viewing, with pauses at appropriate points to give them thinking/processing time. If this is not done there is a danger that the whole recognition system gets clogged up and learners are overwhelmed.

	Girl	Policeman	Man	Woman
Can you help me, please?				
Where's the park?				
On the left				
On the right, etc				

Follow me (BBC)

★ Sequencing/re-arranging activities

These still rely heavily on the recognition of individual words and phrases, whilst moving towards a need for correct comprehension, if the activity is to be successful. At the most basic levels they can be linked to pictures. Students have six pictures in front of them, e.g. a car, a phone, a book, a paper, a bottle and a table. They then listen to the excerpt and have to number the objects in the order in which they are mentioned. More challenging sequencing activities rely on text. Students are given a number of phrases which appear in the sequence, but which are out of order.

e.g. *In a street*

I don't know	2
It's not there	4
Now, where is Castle Street?	1
Yes, it's here on the left	5
Just a minute. Look at the map	3

They can be asked to put them in order first and then to use the video replay as a check. Alternatively, the sequencing can follow the first or second viewing.

It is often a good starting point for exploitation if everybody agrees on what has happened in an excerpt. One way of doing this is to list the events in the order in which they appeared. Here's an example from *At home in Britain* (BBC/EF Colleges)

List the events in the correct order

1. They invite Mr and Mrs Johnson
2. They discuss the menu
3. A photographer takes a photograph
4. They decide to go to a Greek restaurant
5. Two people drop out
6. They order their meal
7. They decide to go to a disco
8. When they arrive home they find Stephen rehearsing
9. They persuade Mikko to go too.

★ Matching activities

These can either be presented in the form of speech bubbles or text. In either case there is a choice as to whether the video is used as a check of what has been done or as the initial prompt for the activity. Students are asked to link the appropriate questions, answers and statements together.

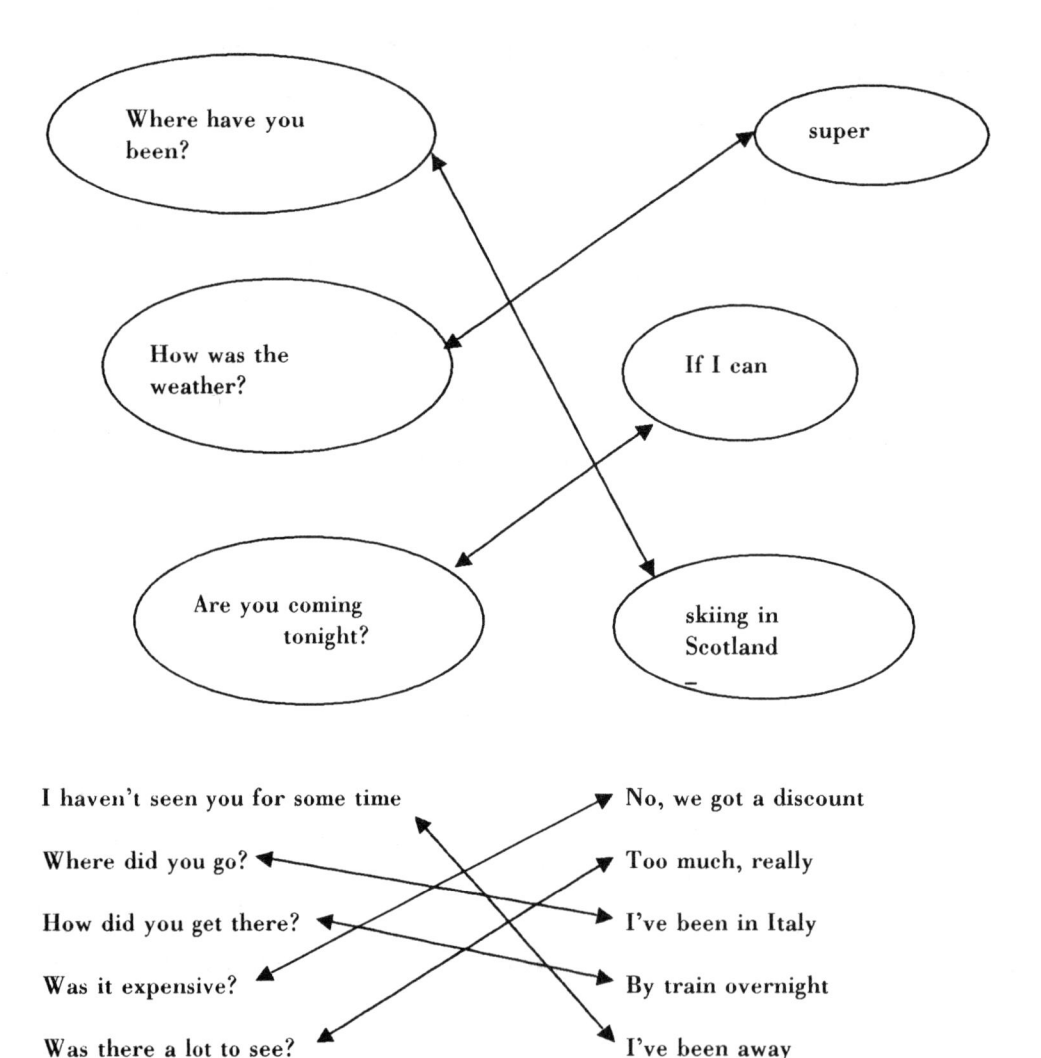

```
  Where have you                          super
     been?

  How was the                           If I can
   weather?

  Are you coming                       skiing in
     tonight?                          Scotland
```

I haven't seen you for some time   No, we got a discount

Where did you go?   Too much, really

How did you get there?   I've been in Italy

Was it expensive?   By train overnight

Was there a lot to see?   I've been away

★ True-false statements

This sort of activity is one of the most familiar. It can be varied by introducing other alternatives such as 'accept/reject' where learners are asked to accept or reject statements on the basis of their accuracy or relevance. But to effect the transfer from text to video-based activity, a number of extra decisions on strategy need to be made.

Here are some of the questions to be asked in order to define the level of difficulty and the nature of the impact made on the student. From these questions it can be seen that there are many ways of varying the presentation and that the role of the teacher is crucial in matching the needs of students to the level of difficulty demanded of them.

Aux magasins

UNIT 7 SCENE B

Olivier and Stéphanie buy some cards, stamps, and a souvenir at the same kiosk.

ACTIVITY 4

Put an X next to the statements below according to whether they are *vrai* or *faux*.

	Vrai	Faux
1. Olivier achète treize cartes.	☐	☐
2. Il veut un timbre pour les États-Unis.	☐	☐
3. Il veut aussi un timbre pour l'Angleterre.	☐	☐
4. Et un pour le Portugal.	☐	☐
5. La vendeuse a beaucoup de souvenirs.	☐	☐
6. Stéphanie achète la tour-eiffel.	☐	☐
7. Elle paie vingt-deux francs.	☐	☐

Breakthrough French (Macmillan)

Some questions of strategy

- At what point are the true-false statements introduced? Before the first viewing? After the first viewing and *en bloc* before the second viewing? Individually during the second viewing and directly associated with the particular language point? Before the second viewing but with learners being asked to make their selections only at the end of the play-back sequence?
- Should the true-false statements be given orally by the teacher, or printed on a worksheet?
- Should the statements be given in the target or native language? (N.B. The latter is not always the easiest.)

★ Multiple choice questions

These, too, are familiar, but the same strategic questions need to be posed as for true-false above. The point at which the question is asked, the mode and the language need to be decided in order to define the level of difficulty for the learner. There are many things wrong with multiple choice as an examination tool, but as a stimulus to effective and purposeful listening they work quite well. It is necessary, though, to ensure that the distractors are genuine and that the level of language in the questions matches (or is easier than) the level of language in the programme.

Quelle heure est-il?

A man inquires about trains from Bordeaux to Paris

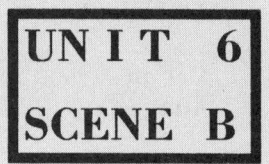

UNIT 6 SCENE B

ACTIVITY 3

Circle the correct answers to the questions below.

1. Il va à Paris
   a. avec deux amis.
   b. seul.
   c. avec son épouse et ses deux enfants.

2. Il cherche
   a. le train le plus pratique.
   b. le plus rapide.
   c. le premier train de la journée.

3. Le voyage à Paris dure
   a. deux heures cinquante-neuf.
   b. douze heures cinquante-neuf.
   c. dix heures.

4. Le prix en seconde classe avec la Carte de Famille est de
   a. neuf cent trente-cinq francs.
   b. six cent vingt-cinq francs.
   c. cinq cent trente francs.

5. En bord le T.G.V. il y a
   a. une voiture-restaurant.
   b. des couchettes.
   c. un wagon-lit.

Breakthrough French (Macmillan)

★ The compilation of lists

At first sight, this activity sounds rather dull, but in practice it can generate interest, particularly if given a competitive edge with students working in pairs, groups or teams. The task here is simply to get learners to spot words which belong to a certain group. There are, basically, three types of list:

- lexical lists where learners are asked to pick out word groups such as *objects that could be found in the kitchen*, *verbs to do with travelling*, and *colours or clothes*;
- functional lists where the task is to note phrases such as *expressing likes or dislikes, ways of being polite, expressing agreement or persuading people to do things*;
- grammatical lists where students spot *question tags*, examples of the *present continuous tense, relative pronouns*, etc.

★ Comparison

There are possibilities for using pictures to support the exploitation of programmes. Some television material is visually very descriptive and lends itself to making up short sentences based on the video vocabulary or asking students to draw what you are saying - a sort of visual dictation. You can give instructions on the furnishing of a room, the location of key buildings, on a town plan, etc. Alternatively, students could be given a number of pictures relating to a programme. You make statements about these pictures and learners have to associate the statement with one of the pictures.

★ Gap-fill

This is a traditional exercise which is given a new dimension when linked to television. With text-based examples, it can be unnatural, often boring, but as a follow-up to a video clip it comes over as more relevant.

At the stationers

Client:	*I'd like some ... paper, please*
Assistant:	*Which kind would you ...?*
Client:	*Airmail, ...?*
Assistant:	*What size would you like? Small or ...?*
Client:	*Small, please. And do you have ...?*

please envelopes writing large like etc.

The point at which the video is paused in gap-fill exercises is important. With short extracts it is probably adequate to ask learners to fill in the gaps at the end of the second viewing. For longer extracts it is often advisable to pause every couple of lines during the second showing and to give learners time to make their selection. It is important, incidentally, to make this exercise one of selection from a jumbled list, rather than asking learners to fill in the gaps from their own knowledge or guesswork. Otherwise too many spelling errors occur and, perversely, it is often the incorrect word spelling which is remembered for future use.

★ Summaries

Whilst, obviously, it is preferable at more advanced levels to ask students for summaries in the target language, there is, at beginners level, still some point in making short summaries in L1 (mother tongue). This can be used as a check on comprehension and as a prelude to more detailed active listening activities.

★ Hands up when you hear ...

This can be used occasionally as a classroom activity to re-energise flagging interest. It can be done in teams, with an independent judge noting who is the first to react to hearing a particular word or phrase. It can be presented either in single words/phrases with the teacher giving the teams instructions to listen out for a single word which will occur in the next thirty seconds. Alternatively, a list of words can be put up on the board or the OHP (overhead projector) and students asked to raise their hands when they hear any of them. At this point, the video is paused and the judge adjudicates.

★ Descriptions

A good way of training students to be aware of paralinguistic features is to use a description grid. This can be done along various lines; it can relate to clothing, to appearance, to personality, to actions, etc. It is a particularly good way of teaching adjectives. For example:

Relate the adjectives to the appropriate person

George		Pam
	surprised	
	in a hurry	
	quiet	
	busy	
	disappointed	
	furious	
	nervous, etc	

Most of the activities described above are meant primarily for basic or lower-intermediate learners. At upper-intermediate and advanced level it is likely that increased use of the target language will be made; with correspondingly less necessity to observe the cautions and credos set out at the start of this chapter. However, there is still a place for activities at advanced level which specifically target listening and, indeed, many of the suggestions (even true-false and lists) can easily be upgraded in difficulty. There are, in addition, a few examples of activities which are of most use at higher levels.

★ Advanced listening grids

An increasingly popular activity is to use the news as a resource. The obvious problem posed for the teacher is the preparation time, or lack of it, necessary to generate worksheets etc. A particularly useful device is to use a standard listening grid that gives a framework for understanding and analysing any bulletin.

Who	What	Where	When	Why	How	Comment
1. The Pope	visit	South America	yesterday	talk to as many people as possible	plane	enthusiastic welcome
2. The President	promised help for stranded whales	Alaska	to-day	?	ice-breaker	time short to save them

The notes, as above, can be written in L1, if L2 (foreign language) is a barrier. To give students time to fill it in, the three-phase approach is best. Phase 1, play it through without a pause. Phase 2, pause after each of the news items for notes to be made. Phase 3, re-play without stopping for reinforcement.

Similar listening grids can be used to good effect with standard courses. Here's one relating to *Challenges* (BBC) where a young girl goes flat-hunting.

	Flat 1	Flat 2	Flat 3
Sharing with how many? Rent per week/month? Cooking arrangements? Items supplied? Shared facilities? Problems? Advantages?			

★ Keyword context questions

In this activity a number of keywords are selected and given to the students in advance. During the second viewing, the video is paused at the end of a sentence in which a word appears. Students are then asked either to quote the exact linguistic context in which the word was used, or to explain in L1 the way in which it was used.

If, in a sentence such as: *The helicopter landed on the pad just in time to save the girl's life*, 'pad' is selected as the keyword, students would either have to quote the rest of the sentence or to explain that 'pad' is a specialist term for where a helicopter lands.

★ Translation

Although translation is not encouraged by many teachers, it is nevertheless often considered by learners as being a useful way of practising and cementing the language. When translation is being introduced to learners it can be stressed that what is being sought is not an exact word-for-word translation, but rather 'find the equivalent for'. To make the most of this, the three-phase approach should be used with pauses during the second viewing at points appropriate for translation. This brings the activity to life in a way that was rarely possible in the days of text-based translation work.

★ Re-translation

This is perhaps more palatable to those who are wary of translation. Here, students are given a number of target phrases in L1. Their task in appropriate pauses during the second showing is to locate the equivalent phrase in the target language. Again, this sparks off a lot of active involvement based on purposeful listening and it can be extremely valuable for developing aural acuity and vocabulary power.

The activities described above are by no means exhaustive, nor, of course, do they represent any kind of dogma. They do, however, serve to illustrate how versatile video can be and also how it is possible to generate useful work which focuses specifically on the development of listening power. Having discussed the value of video for generalising listening activities, we can now turn to the ways in which the medium can support active oral work.

CHAPTER THREE

Using video to develop spoken skills

Most students, when asked what they want to do with their language skills, indicate 'speaking' as the most important function. In a recent survey into BBC courses, some 60% of the adults questioned as they embarked on the course indicated that this was what they most hoped to be able to do. When surveyed afterwards, most were reasonably happy with the course, but were very guarded as to what they had achieved.

Most teachers, too, stress that giving pupils a good oral ability is one of, if not **the** prime objective of their courses. Many insist on L2 only within their classes and take oral responses as the prime indicator of the success of a lesson. This emphasis may well be practical and successful in some cases, but a cautionary note needs to be sounded.

Oral fluency is indisputably a key terminal objective but we need to be sure that we don't demand too much too soon. In large groups of pupils there is a limit on how much any individual can say within a lesson, particularly when the peer group is not that supportive. There is also considerable evidence to suggest that learners will begin to speak when they are ready and that to force it too quickly in unnatural situations actually impedes progress. A little achieved successfully is, in general, better than setting up unrealistic expectations that made learners feel they are 'failing'. The maintenance of confidence, confidence in the teacher, in the course and in the learner's own ability is a crucial factor in sustaining motivation and achieving a satisfying level of language proficiency. We must never forget that people often find effective oral communication difficult in their native tongue and that whether or not they are comfortable talking in a foreign language often has more to do with their own personality (whether, for instance, they are shy or extrovert) than with the characteristics of a language course or a teacher's style. It is also true that too much time is spent by learners listening to other people's 'bad' language when, perversely, incorrect models may become as firmly established as the correct ones.

This note of caution should not, however, be taken to indicate that there is any doubt about the ability of video to play a significant role in the development of oral skills. If anything, the converse is true. When carefully and sympathetically handled, video can provide a whole range of stimuli which provoke active oral work more effectively than any other means. There are numerous activities that can be introduced.

★ Repetition

This is probably the best starting point for oral work. It allows learners to perform in a non-threatening environment and gives them an opportunity to begin getting their tongues around some of the strange sounds and rhythms of the new language. Video is ideal for presenting a range of speech models from different sexes, different ages, different backgrounds, different situations. Learners can associate the phrase to be repeated with a person or with an identifiable visual context on the screen and this makes for additional and effective motivation *vis à vis* work based on text or sound-only sources. A lot of valuable fun can be generated when repetition focuses not just on the words themselves and the accent but also on the tone of voice used by the model speakers.

In introducing repetition work, the teacher should be aware of the big difference created when s/he intervenes in the process. If pupils are asked to repeat direct from the screen, it is clearly more difficult than when the video is paused and the teacher repeats the phrase before asking the class or the individual to respond. This 'sanitisation' of the language to be spoken is not necessarily right or wrong, it is just important that the teacher recognises the effect of intervention and has used his/her professional judgment in deciding to do it or not to do it.

★ Predictive speech

This is one of the most useful and compelling of techniques to adopt. There are, basically, two forms of the activity; predictive speech recall which is 'closed' and predictive speech 'pure' which is open-ended.

In the former, a short clip (ten seconds) is shown during the second run-through. The video is then re-wound and paused at an appropriate point. The group (or individuals) are then invited to recall what is said next and the pause released as a check on whether they were correct. This directly links purposeful listening with a controlled oral response. In accepting or rejecting suggestions, it is as important that you place emphasis on **how** something is said (tone, stress, feeling, etc) as on **what** is said. As in many of the activities suggested in this chapter, learners can be encouraged to work in pairs, making their predictions to each other rather than to the class as a whole. This gives more opportunity for individual practice, though it does limit the amount of monitoring and correction that the teacher can undertake.

In the second type of prediction (pure), the video is paused and the group is invited to speculate on what will be said next. This is obviously open-ended with no correct or incorrect version. Success is judged entirely on whether learners have been sufficiently stimulated to say something. It is a good activity for mixed-ability groups, since both modest and complex suggestions can be accepted equally.

Prediction works particularly well, incidentally, with advertisements. Most learners find advertisements attractive and intrinsically motivating and they provide a rich source of authentic material accessible even at beginners' level. The best strategy is to choose advertisements where the product is not immediately clear and to play the clip for a few seconds before pausing and asking learners to speculate on what it is about and, perhaps, what makes them think that. Pausing can often be repeated two or three times before all is revealed and it can provide a lot of fun, not to mention valuable language practice, *en route*.

★ Sound-down/sound-only activities

There are a variety of activities that can be introduced by taking out either the sound or the vision and inviting speculation as to what is being said or what is being shown. As with 'prediction', this can be done as a recall task or it can be done during the first showing. It can be done with pairs or small groups working together and negotiating what to suggest, or as a class activity. However it is introduced, it is important not to select clips which are too long, particularly for beginners. Sixty seconds of television is a long time when it is being put under the microscope in this way.

★ Information-gap activities

Here again there are a number of ways in which these can be presented to learners. Perhaps the simplest technique is to select a short excerpt (one to three minutes) which has no speech, just mood music. At the beginning of *Sherlock Holmes* (Longman EFL Video), for instance, there is a two-minute sequence over which the title credits are given and where, in the steaming streets of pre-war London, a man is found by a bobby stabbed to death clutching Holmes' address. To exploit this the class are divided into pairs and they decide which one will view and which one will turn away from the screen (the music here is particularly evocative). Then those who did see it are asked to describe what happened, prompted by questions of clarification from those who had their backs to the screen. If time allows, the non-viewers can be invited to speculate on what they think happened before the description starts. This sort of activity always gets learners involved and gives them a genuine interest in expressing themselves in the foreign language. Although it is preferable to give the people who are not viewing some non-verbal clues in the form of sound effects or music, the same activity can be successful with the sound down and no music or sound effects.

★ Jigsaw activities

Another way of exploiting information-gap activities is for the class to split up, with each part viewing a different sequence from the same programme. They then come together in pairs and explain to each other what they have seen. Role cards can also be used to advantage. Here the whole class views an excerpt and then breaks up into pairs. Each person has a role card but with different information or topics to explore. The cards are used as cues for a structured discussion or actual role-play based on the common viewing experience.

★ Learner originated question work

It is clearly just as important to give learners experience of asking as of answering questions. One way of using video to stimulate this, is to pause the programme frequently during the second showing and to invite questions based on what has just been seen or heard, with any type of question allowed. When this activity is first introduced the questions can be from an individual within the group and directed at the teacher. The class then gets a feel for the way in which the questions should be answered (i.e. not just yes/no, but as fully as possible). When sufficient models have been given, the activity can be handed over to pairs with the brief to ask and answer questions of each other until the pause is released.

As an alternative, a sequence can be shown a couple of times, perhaps using 'exploded viewing' on the second showing where the teacher pauses the tape occasionally and says nothing. The task for the learner is to prepare a number of questions which are all asked and answered in pairs at the end of the sequence. This gives learners a little more time than the spontaneous questioning and a higher standard of accuracy, together with more 'insightful' questioning, can be expected.

★ Synonym work

This is handled in the same way as the previous activity. The difference being that every time the video is paused, learners are asked to find synonyms, alternative ways of expressing the same idea. Experience has shown that this is a popular activity which gets learners involved and it certainly helps to promote mental agility and to improve their ability to process and manipulate the language.

★ Stop-frame descriptions

Video players are increasingly available which have an accurate and solid freeze-frame when paused. This opens the way to a simple but effective oral activity which can be instituted at any time to give learners a mental jolt, or it can be part of a planned strategy. When the video is paused learners are simply asked to say anything that comes to mind which is sparked off by the image on the screen. At first this can produce simple descriptions - *There is a man and a boy*, etc - but learners respond readily to encouragement to be a bit more adventurous. Comments relating to what people are thinking or to relationships soon begin to appear. Stop-frame description is a popular activity which is particularly useful for mixed-ability classes. It enables all members of the group to feel a sense of achievement and to participate whether with a simple or a more complex utterance in the present, future or past tense. It can be presented as a class activity or used for pair work. A competitive edge can be added by having two teams and seeing which team can make the most statements for each stop-frame.

★ Speculation

There is a lot of mileage in encouraging learners to speculate. Again, this gives them a free rein and stimulates a wide range of reactions. Speculation can be introduced like the stop-frame activity above at any time during a showing to keep people on their toes, or it can form the basis of a more structured discussion at the end of a three or four minutes sequence. There are many devices to spark off speculation: learners can be asked what further questions they might have put to a character, why somebody looks as he/she does, where he/she is going, etc. Reflecting on a whole sequence, they can be asked to speculate on longer term issues such as what might have happened to a character in a year's time, how a situation might develop or what the consequences of actions might be. The exact format of the speculation-prompts depends of course, on the nature of the material, but the range of possibilities is virtually endless. It is certainly sometimes surprising how creative and imaginative learners can be when they are given their freedom.

★ Retrospective questioning

There is some evidence to suggest that the most frequent video-related activity to be found is retrospective questioning by the teacher. Here the teacher, armed with a transcript or with previous knowledge of a programme, peppers the class with questions. Learners are thus expected to have first understood and then to have memorised a substantial amount of information. They are put on the spot by the teacher and invited to remember sometimes quite obscure, or at least insignificant facts, and to express those facts fluently and accurately with a good accent and correct intonation.

This is, perhaps, the most dangerous activity to link to video in that it can so easily destroy an individual's confidence. The pressure to produce an answer in front of an often unsupportive peer group to an authoritarian teacher often proves too daunting. The anxiety is lessened to some extent if the questions to be answered are given before the sequence is viewed and if the tape is paused at appropriate points as a signal to learners that they should be paying special attention to what has just been said (or seen). However, teacher-originated question work should be approached with great caution.

Far less threatening is to hand over the job of inventing questions to the learners themselves. They can be asked, for instance, to view a short sequence and then to be given time to formulate four or five questions. These questions can be directed at other members of the class, at the teacher or used as the basis for a few minutes pair work. On the first occasions this activity is introduced, it is a good idea to set up models and to give examples of both questions and answers. In this way learners can be encouraged to ask questions that reflect not just **what** is said, but **how**, thus focusing attention more precisely on the language than on often unimportant scraps of information. *How did the policeman reply to the tourist?* is a better question than *What number bus did the tourist have to catch?* Model answers can also help to point out the value of expanding a bit in order to make what you say more interesting. A response of *yes* to the question *Has Peter any brothers and sisters?* is obviously less satisfactory than *Yes, he's got an elder sister called Sue and a younger brother who's twelve called Nicky.*

★ Dialogue frames

A good way of reinforcing recall of key phrases and structures is to use a simple dialogue frame as a prompt for controlled oral responses. After viewing a sequence, a frame can be put up on the OHP with words which lead to the expression of phrases or sentences. They have the advantage of being very quick to produce - and anything which limits the amount of teacher preparation time must be considered a plus - and yet they are effective. An exchange which went like this:

Jonathan:	*Oh, hello! I didn't expect to see you*
Jane:	*I was just passing, so I thought I'd pop in*
Jonathan:	*That's nice. Do you want a coffee?*
Jane:	*Mm, I'm thirsty, I haven't had a drink since breakfast*
Jonathan:	*Aren't you working today?*
Jane:	*No, I'm taking the day off*
Jonathan:	*Are you doing anything exciting?*
Jane:	*I don't know about exciting, I need some new clothes*

could then be presented to the class like this:

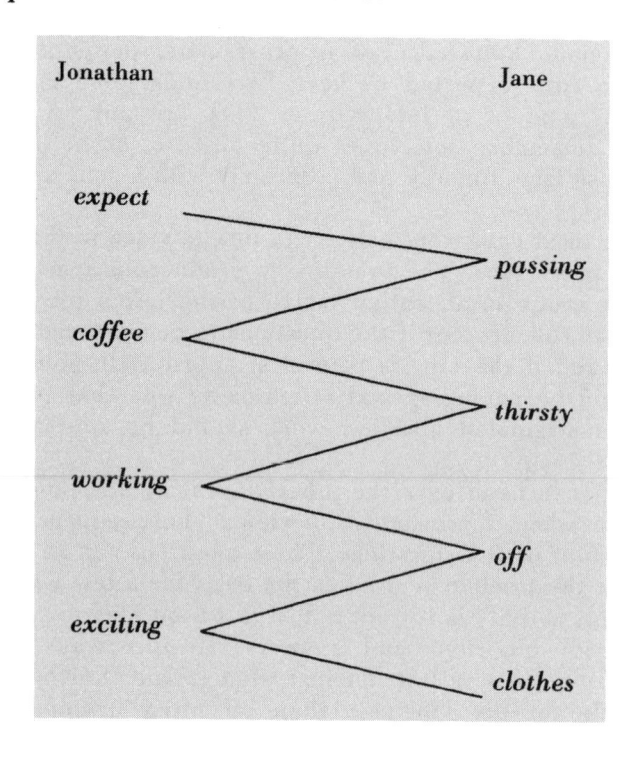

Jonathan   Jane

expect

           passing

coffee

           thirsty

working

           off

exciting

           clothes

Using this format it is relatively easy to reconstruct the exchange, to reinforce some useful linguistic gems and, of course, to expand from it with questions such as *How else could Jane have answered?* or *What do you think Jane does?* or *What's a synonym for: 'I need some new clothes'?* Techniques such as this help increase word power, improve learners' ability to manipulate the language and build up confidence.

★ Mime cues

Not every group will initially take to this activity, but it will appeal to groups of an extrovert and co-operative disposition. Mime cues are best used sparingly, but they do provide an alternative, increasing the variety of devices to stimulate active oral work. Mime work is best introduced when learners have seen a number of programmes in a series or at least have been exposed to a video with several different, easily identifiable scenes in it. Ask for or select a couple of volunteers from the group and ask them to go outside for a few minutes and invent a scene. They then return to the class and proceed to mime their selected scene as though it were a series of stills. They 'freeze', therefore, at appropriate places and only carry on when somebody in the class has come up with the words from the video which express what they are portraying in their frozen tableau. With the right group, this can produce some amusing and enjoyable moments, whilst still providing an effective learning experience.

Many of the ideas set out above can be adapted for use at a variety of levels from beginners to advanced. There are, however, a number of activities which are best introduced to more advanced students, since they demand a higher degree of language manipulation, a wider vocabulary, a more precise knowledge of structure or the ability to express yourself in a series of connected or coherent sentences.

★ Re-use of keywords or phrases

This activity can be linked to keyword context questions already discussed in the previous chapter on developing listening skills. Here, learners are asked to extend the contexts in which the keywords have been used. If, for instance, the keyword was 'pad' in the phrase *The helicopter touched down on the landing pad*, learners are asked to come up with other sentences using 'pad' (or derivatives from it). In this instance, it could produce quite a long list of suggestions such as *Could you pass me the writing pad, please? The astronauts walked onto the launch pad; The student padded out his work with lots of irrelevant information;* or *The dog padded quietly into the room.*

★ Chaining

Chaining is a good way of adding some interest to a lesson, whilst developing mental agility and reinforcing vocabulary. It involves re-telling a story or recounting the sequence of what has been seen. Students are asked one after another to contribute. The way in which the 'buck' passes within the group can vary. The teacher can act as the conductor, simply pointing to members of the class and changing at appropriate moments the person who is being asked to re-tell what has happened. The change can also be at the learner's instigation, when one person thinks s/he has said enough, he simply points to somebody else who has to carry on. Chaining can also be given a competitive edge by having two teams. Member A of Team 1 begins and then hands over to member A of Team 2. Whenever there is hesitation or deviation, the opposing team can challenge. If the teacher (or a neutral judge selected from the class) thinks the challenge is correct, a point is added. The team with the fewest points at the end of the story is the 'winner'.

Whatever the format, a re-told story might look like this:

> Michael had been out late (*pass*)
> at a dance and (*pass*)
> was feeling very tired. The others had decided (*pass*)
> it was his turn to (*pass*)
> do the shopping (*pass*)
> He said (*pass*)
> he was feeling too ill and there was no way (*pass*)
> he was going out shopping (*pass*) etc, etc.

★ Commentary work

There are, basically, two types of commentary work. The first is where learners are asked to give a commentary to a film they have already seen which involves primarily re-calling and expressing what they have understood. The second is more open-ended, with learners being asked to work out a commentary to match the visuals but without their first having heard the original sound-track.

Whichever mode is adopted, there are a few important points to bear in mind. The sequence on which the commentary is based should be fairly short. Two to three minutes is usually enough to provide work for an hour. Material which avoids dialogues or interviews is most appropriate, particularly if there is a lot of explicit visual movement so that the links between what is seen and what is said, or could be said, are firmly established. Commentary work requires a lot of teacher support, particularly on the first few occasions it is tried. This support can take the form of working with the class, using the pause button to elicit suggestions which are then written up. Or it could be that learners are given a number of key phrases and cues which they use as a framework on which to construct their own commentary. Since this is a very demanding activity the importance of thorough preparation cannot be overestimated, if learners are to make the most of it and not to feel the task is beyond them. The aim should be participation in the activity and not adjudication of individual performances.

Although commentary work can be instigated with the whole class, it is best tackled in the language lab. Show the excerpt through once for general orientation and again with pauses to allow students to make notes and to stress key vocabulary. Then give learners time (five to ten minutes) to assemble their thoughts and to prepare themselves. Show the sequence a third time (if possible initially just slightly slowed down) and ask them to record their own commentary. A touch of sophistication can be given from the console by bringing up music or sound effects where there is no speech and recording that onto the students' master track. Once the commentary is made, students can watch the video again and listen to what they have said. There is then further scope, if time allows, for playing some of the individual students' versions to the whole group, for comment or analysis.

If the learner is reasonably pleased with the commentary, it acts as a real boost to confidence and this type of activity whether in the 'recall' or the 'pure' mode is excellent for building up accurate oral fluency.

★ Role-play

Role-play is an example of another activity which can bring fun and variety into the language classroom, but which also needs careful handling if it is not to fall flat. In situations where the peer group is unsupportive, for whatever reason, it may be best avoided. However, there are enough examples of success to make it worth consideration.

One thing is sure. If role-play is likely to work at all it will do so when based on video. A major problem with 'cold' role-play is that learners not only have to cope with the demands of the foreign language, but they also have to be imaginative enough to create their own situations and plots. When role-play is based on a common viewing experience, a clear context is provided into which language work can be built, but one in which there is still scope for individual invention and initiative.

The way role-play is actually handled obviously depends on the nature of the group and of the material. Whatever the strategy employed, however, a golden rule is to allow time for preparation before performance. This may detract a little from the spontaneity of the performance, but the act of preparation is itself linguistically valuable and learners are likely to feel far less pressure if they are given adequate time to work on what they are going to say.

A good way of handling role-play is to select a programme that has a number of short, clearly definable sequences. It is usually appropriate to work in some comprehension activities during the second play-back to ensure adequate understanding of the material before going on to active production. When this stage has been reached, the class can be divided into groups with each group allotted a different sequence. The sequences are then prepared and 'performed', followed by such comment and analysis from the teacher as is appropriate. It is important that role-play doesn't go on too long, if it is not to become boring, so the selection of material with snappy sequences and plenty of impact is crucial. The re-enacting of detective films such as *Sherlock Holmes* or *Maigret* is particularly appropriate in this context.

★ Stepped recall

In many video or television courses, as opposed to authentic television material, the language has been carefully scripted to reflect the specific needs of language learners. It is therefore valuable to achieve a level of familiarity with the script which can lead to oral production.

One way of promoting this is to use the text of the programmes as a prop, and as the activity progresses, to step up the amount of recall required by individual students. To achieve this, divide the class into pairs or, if appropriate to the scene being studied, into small groups. Each learner is given a copy of the transcript and this is then used as the basis for the activity. If working in pairs, both students are allowed to have the transcript and they read through it together, taking on the roles of the television characters. The scene is then performed a second time but, on this occasion, student B is not allowed to read the transcript. On a third run-through student A has to work without the transcript, but student B has it. Finally, the scene is spoken by both students, neither of whom has access to the transcript. This procedure, modified as necessary to reflect the number of characters in the original scene, promotes the assimilation and retention of key language exchanges.

It is, perhaps, important at this stage to explain that the reason 'reading' has not been given a separate chapter is that many of the activities suggested above do implicitly involve reading the language. Experience has shown that an understanding of the spoken and of the printed/written word is closely linked. Thus a strategy which places stress on active listening and oral activities will produce students who are also able to read the language, even if they have been exposed to only a limited number of explicit reading tasks. There is, in fact, evidence to suggest that many people spend more time reading the foreign language than listening, speaking or writing it. There is, therefore, every reason to monitor the development of this skill closely, but as indicated above, it seems possible to enhance reading ability by ensuring students have a good passive understanding of the spoken language and relying on the inevitable occurrence of written/printed language within other activities to develop reading ability, almost as a by-product.

★ The preparation of TV programmes

A logical extension of using professionally prepared videos as the basis for language work, is to encourage students to make their own material. This will be handled in more detail in another book in the series on using the video camera, so it is not appropriate to go into detail here.

However, it is worth signalling that groups who become familiar with the use of video often find the transition to producing material relatively easy. A 'Television Production Workshop' provides a realistic, effective and popular way of acquiring and practising communicative skills. In a 'Television Workshop', the end result is comparatively unimportant. Television is used here primarily as a catalyst for language work, rather than as a medium for presenting it. There is an unlimited range of formats and programme themes which can be used, but the essence of the exercise is that in preparing their own television material, learners become actively involved in key communicative activities such as asking and answering questions, persuading someone to do something, negotiating, telephoning, summarising texts and sound material, writing scripts, speaking the language in a controlled environment, etc.

Very little training is necessary for this sort of 'in-house' production and it can be readily adapted to the time available. At one end of the scale the TV programme might involve little more than taking part in a discussion, though at a more complex level the final programme can have many of the features of 'real' television with titles, graphics, photos, film inserts, etc.

Making programmes is exciting and it certainly motivates the majority of students to get involved in using the language. It presents, additionally, an interesting challenge for the teacher and can lead to the introduction of new approaches and to a re-evaluation of his/her own role. There is, however, a big danger which lies in wait once the programme has been recorded. The way in which the material is analysed is crucially important. If the teacher uses the video just as evidence to illustrate mistakes, this can easily destroy learners' confidence. Not everybody enjoys seeing himself on television and a careful, sympathetic touch is necessary. It is usually preferable to use the 'pause' to point to successful examples of language use - *Did you hear what she said there? Terrific; Notice the way Angie is smiling when she speaks and how she appears relaxed; That was a good answer, wasn't it?* In this way, learners come to see the making of programmes as a natural extension of classroom work and they overcome their inhibitions; a 'victory', incidentally, which is readily translated into other aspects of their everyday lives and which can help make learners more effective communicators in their own as well as in the target language.

The suggestions outlined above are by no means exhaustive, but they serve to illustrate the tremendous flexibility of the medium and the crucial role of the teacher. Not all suggestions will suit all classes, but there is a sufficient range to show that television is not a soporific and that as a teacher builds up his or her own confidence and competence in handling video, so the medium will become an ever more important and effective part of everyday language teaching weaponry.

Before moving on to look at the development of written skills in the next chapter, it is pertinent to interject a few thoughts on error correction. This is clearly a difficult area with a constant tension between the need to boost confidence and encourage fluency on the one hand, and the feeling that you are doing the student no favours by allowing repeated errors to go unchecked on the other.

The answer as to whether to correct or not obviously rests ultimately with the professional judgment of the teacher. The view adopted in this taxonomy of activities is that, on balance, it is better to put the stress on prevention rather than cure and to ensure that wherever possible, sufficient groundwork and preparation has been done to, at least, give learners a fair chance of getting it right. There is also an underlying presumption that the more learners are exposed to 'correct' language, the more likely they are to produce it. Spending too much time analysing mistakes can sometimes, perversely, only serve to ensure that it is the incorrect rather than the correct item of language that finds its way into the linguistic memory. If correction is necessary, it is better done by briefly replacing the bad with a good model, otherwise there is a danger that learners will build up a resistance to speaking at all. The most important factor is: Has the learner at least succeeded in getting the message across?' If not, corrective help is necessary, but, if so, a pat on the back is likely to produce better long-term results. We often underestimate the difficulty learners have in speaking the language, particularly when participating in activities based on video until they have become really familiar with the medium. Intervention by the teacher to correct spoken errors should, therefore, be kept to the minimum and stress placed on positive reinforcement to make sure the video is regarded as a friend and not as a stick to beat linguistic competence into learners or as a mirror of their painstaking inadequacies.

CHAPTER FOUR

Using video to develop written skills

Owing to the nature of the medium, many people assume that the prime use of video is in the development of oral and aural skills. In fact, it also has a big contribution to make enhancing written skills. Exercises and activities that are familiarly linked to text can often be adapted to follow up and reinforce television work. When asked why they do not use video, some teachers indicate a feeling that it is not 'serious' enough, that the pressures of exam work mean they have no time for what they see as a peripheral resource. In practice, television can be just as effective as text in stimulating a wide range of useful, main-stream written activities, with the added bonus that television can provide an exemplar which is likely to be more motivating and to offer a more comprehensible and realistic starting point due to the contextualising visual dimension.

More people than ever before are likely to be called upon to craft sentences in the course of their work, and television has a big role to play in helping with T S Eliot's *intolerable wrestle with words and meaning*. At basic level, this might mean little more than the selection of appropriate words and their accurate transcription, or getting a pen around unfamiliar words and symbols. At more advanced levels, television can stimulate the succinct and structured expression of coherent thoughts.

★ Working with jumbles and clues

Transposing into written work the axiom that learners should not be asked to take part in activities or to do exercises for which they have not been thoroughly prepared and that, whatever they do, there should be a high chance of getting it right, the opportunities for written work at beginners' level are clearly limited. There is, however, some value in letting learners write in carefully controlled situations, particularly for those who feel that writing a word helps them remember it.

Exercises with jumbled answers, word soups and clue letters all achieve this purpose. They are familiar, but given a useful new dimension when linked to excerpts from television.

A word soup

Here are thirteen words to do with eating in a restaurant in a word soup. See if you can spot them and write them out. They were all used in the excerpt you saw.

dessert .....mousse .....dish .....pastry .....fish .....pie .....food .....sauces ..... kidney..... steak .....meat .....tasty .....menu

```
V D O O F F U P
M E G D I S H Y
O Y R T S A P T
U E E T H U T S
S N A R A C I A
S D E S S E R T
E I A M N S M I
P K A E T S S M
```

Many of the suggestions in Chapter 2 relating to listening practice can be adapted to provide basic written activities - sequencing, re-arranging dialogues into the correct order, compilation of lists, exploitation of pictures, gap-fill are obvious candidates for re-presentation with the emphasis on the written form.

Some learners enjoy crosswords or word-games and there is potential for introducing these in virtually every television sequence. They can be set up at basic level with jumbled answers or introduced by the teacher who makes sure the words are known before learners start. If the simple pattern shown below is used, there is sufficient flexibility of format to enable the word box to be very quickly created by the teacher.

As an alternative, it is possible to get learners to work in pairs or small groups actually creating the clues and the word boxes. These are then checked by the teacher before handing them over to another pair or group to complete. This introduces a stimulating new dimension to the activity for the learner (whilst saving the teacher valuable preparation time).

Use the clues to fill in the word boxes. When you've done it, the vertical line should give you something tasty for breakfast.

1. A hot drink but not tea or coffee.
2. An alternative to orange?
3. What Catrine orders.
4. You say this when the waiter brings the drink.
5. You're thirsty. J'ai ...
6. Eaten instead of ice-cream.
7. Stephanie ordered a chocolate and vanilla one.
8. Fifty.
9. The last word of 'please' in French.

1.					C	h	o	c	o	l	a	t
2.		c	i	t	r	o	n			
3.					o	r	a	n	g	i	n	a
4.	m	e	r	c	i					
5.					s	o	i	f		
6.					s	o	r	b	e	t	
7.			g	l	a	c	e			
8.			c	i	n	q	u	a	n	t	e
9.	p	l	a	i	t					

(From *Vidéo Passeport Français*)

★ Simple sentences

After the manipulation of single words or exercises requiring selection and transcription of pre-digested text, the next stage is to give learners the opportunity of producing their own language. The filling-in of identity cards, registration forms, responses to adverts, customs declarations, etc is a good starting point, which soon leads on to the writing of post-cards and simple letters.

A popular written activity is to set up a variation of the consequences game. Each person first writes down, say, six questions, with enough space left below them for an answer. The paper is then folded in six and passed on to the next person in the group to answer the first question. The sheet then continues to be passed around until all six questions have been answered. It is then returned to the original writer to read the answers s/he has received. This can obviously be taken further, if appropriate, by getting each student to read out the various questions and their responses to the rest of the group.

The same technique, or simplified versions of it, can also be used for keyword context work (see Chapter 2, p17). Here the prompt is not a question, but a keyword from the programme. The task is then to supply the rest of the phrase in which the keyword appears or, at least, to supply a phrase which makes sense and which shows that the word has been understood.

Jam　　　　　　　*The traffic jam stretched back for three miles*

Lines　　　　　　*The van was parked on double yellow lines*

Meter　　　　　　*The parking meter attendant got out his book*

★ Proof correction

This is a useful activity which relates to the real world of work outside the classroom and which trains aural acuity and the ability to listen accurately, whilst also providing an opportunity for written expression.

Select a short sequence (one to two minutes) from the programme and prepare a slightly amended transcript. The amendments should not introduce grammatical errors, but rather omissions, additions and logical modifications to the text.

On the second run-through, pause the video occasionally to let the words sink in and to let learners mark where they notice any discrepancies between what they hear and what they read. Then ask the group to make the necessary corrections, before playing the video a third time as a check. As well as being 'realistic' and valuable training in itself, proof correction activities help develop accurate written expression.

The solar energy car
(*original transcript*)

Well, we have all heard of a diesel car, an electric car, even a gas-powered car, but a car that is run on sunshine is something else again. Nevertheless, a team of engineers from Berkshire have built a solar-powered machine that does just that, and what's more they are planning to drive it right across Europe, all the way from Athens in Greece to Lisbon in Portugal. Rob Widdow reports:

The solar energy car
(*amended transcript*)

Well, we have all <u>read</u> of a diesel car, an electric car, even a gas car, but a car that is powered by sunshine is something else. Nevertheless, a team of <u>auto</u> engineers from <u>Buckinghamshire</u> have built a solar-powered <u>vehicle</u> that does just that, and what's more they're <u>going</u> to drive it <u>through</u> Europe, <u>from</u> Athens in Greece to Lisbon in Portugal. Rob Widdow <u>demonstrates</u>:

(From *Video Report*)

★ Dictations

Although currently not highly fashionable, dictations can be given a new lease of life when linked to a TV excerpt. The main criticisms of dictations, that they are unnatural, boring and unpopular are, to a large extent, overcome when they are based on authentic language that has been contextualised by the addition of an attractive visual element.

It is preferable to select a connected piece of speech such as a commentary or the introduction to a report rather than a dialogue. It is also important to choose a short excerpt (two minutes = 240 words) if it is not to become unwieldy.

Show the video clip through once or, possibly, twice for orientation and contextualisation. This is to enable learners to understand the gist of what they are going to be faced with and to mark mentally some of the key phrases or words. In the next phase the teacher reads aloud the exploded version in the 'traditional' manner and the learners write down what they heard. There is then a final playback of the clip for reinforcement, with students being given a few minutes to work on any final corrections.

This strategy provides added motivation to tackle what can be a rather arid exercise. Learners are more willing to succumb to the dictation format when it is based on television and thus they benefit from the practice of making specific links between what they hear and what they write.

A specimen dictation

Mr Couttes   My wife heard a noise/in the kitchen/which is across the hall/and opposite our bedroom/and so she went outside/and put the light on./ She found a man there/with a torch/and he immediately attacked her/to prevent her/from making a noise./I jumped out onto the bed/and just bodily fell on him/and we both fell to the floor./He went out of the bedroom/and closed the door.

(Extract from *Video Report*)

★ Completion of a script

A popular activity which integrates the four skills and which produces a written product is script completion. Following comprehension work on the first part of a scene, learners are asked to speculate on what happened next and to produce their own script.

Script completion can be introduced at a relatively early stage, or, of course, it can provide a testing task for advanced learners. The determinants are the level of the source material and the amount of support given by the teacher. At one extreme, learners can be given virtually the whole of the second part of a script in jumbled form and invited to re-write it logically. At the other, they can be set to work following only a brief discussion and a few clue suggestions as to how events might develop.

This activity can be given for homework to be completed individually or, preferably, be the focus for group work where learners negotiate with each other. It is important that the class is not made to feel that there is a 'right' or a 'wrong' answer, but rather that they are being marked more generally on their understanding of the first part of the scene, on correct language and on hints of originality.

The selection of the material and the point at which it is stopped is clearly important if the activity is to be a success. Scenes with relatively few characters and a strong plot, as in detective stories, are usually preferable, but the technique can be applied to more prosaic functional activities such as 'asking the way' or 'ordering a meal'.

★ Parallel scripts

A more structured variation of the same exercise is the creation of parallel scripts. Here learners are shown the whole of a short scene and then invited to re-create it using different vocabulary. There is, therefore, an agreed context with a defined set of characters and action which forms the basis of a communal viewing experience.

Again, it is preferable to select material with relatively few characters and to have a self-contained and clearly defined action.

The advantage of parallel script-writing is that imaginative enthusiasm does not have to extend beyond the learners' linguistic limits and there is a framework on which to hang subsequent analysis and comparisons. It is also suitable both for individual and for small group work.

Specimen extract for parallel script from Video Report

Face of the year
(*Original*)

Liz Wickham	*Are the other girls jealous in your class?*
Lisa Butcher	*No, they're just happy for me. We just laugh about it and they think it's really great.*
Liz Wickham	*Now you're doing 'O' levels at the moment. What do you intend to do seriously when you leave school?*

Lisa Butcher	*Well it changes every day. I'd like to do something with fashion designing or jewellery designing, something like that. Or maybe modelling. Well, it depends how far I get with this, if I get right to the top I'll carry on with it.*

Face of the year
(Possible parallel version)

Liz Wickham	*Do the other girls mind your having been selected?*
Lisa Butcher	*Not really, they're pleased for me. We joke about it and they think it's terrific.*
Liz Wickham	*You're in the middle of exams at the moment. What do you want to be when you leave school?*
Lisa Butcher	*Well, it changes all the time. I'd like to do some designing, fashion designing or jewellery - something on those lines. Or, perhaps, try modelling. Obviously it depends what happens with this. If I win, I'll carry on.*

★ Transcriptions

As a more media-related alternative to dictations at advanced level, the preparation of transcripts is highly demanding, excellent training for developing aural acuity and a good way of building up an awareness of grammatical accuracy in the written mode.

The strategy adopted will depend on the needs of the group and on technical limitations, but, if possible, it is preferable to introduce transcription via the language laboratory or to set it as homework. A short video clip is selected and shown once (or twice) for orientation. Learners are then given an audio cassette on which the sound-track has been recorded and are asked to produce an accurate transcript. The sound prompts the recall of visual images thus aiding comprehension and the linking of transcription to television produces a more stimulating, motivating task than if learners were asked to reproduce the sound-track of an audio tape 'cold'.

In many cases, the sound source from the television or video recorder can be routed directly into the language laboratory to produce the follow-up audio recording. Where this is not possible, recordings can be made via a cable from the sound output of a television set onto a tape recorder or, provided the ambient sound is carefully controlled, even recorded onto tape via a microphone. (This latter mode is not ideal, but where the television is not fitted with a separate sound output socket it does provide an acceptable alternative.)

★ Translation and re-translation work

Although frowned upon in some quarters, translation and re-translation can be valid and even popular activities when used in moderation and in conjunction with the other more communicative work already described. Translation is from L2 to L1; re-translation from L1 to L2.

It is a paradox of education that the activities defined by 'educationalists' as being of limited value or even harmful are often those which learners themselves perceive as being most useful. Many learners, perversely, actually enjoy doing translation, particularly where it is linked to a television sequence that has introduced the language in a realistic setting. It can be presented to students as a reinforcement to listening comprehension or oral work in the form of selected key sentences for translation. Aided by recall of the context of the television programme they have already seen, learners can usually approach the task with more confidence than with traditional translation based on the printed text alone.

Alternatively, translation (or re-translation) can be presented as an exercise in consecutive written interpreting. In this mode, a third person summary is prepared of the television sequence that has already been the subject of oral or listening activities. The complete summary is read out once, then a second time broken up into manageable chunks for learners to write down a translation of what they hear as though in a dictation. The summary is read a third time in its complete form for reinforcement. As a rough guide, two hundred words are enough as the basis for forty-five minutes' work. The learners' scripts can then be collected and marked, or they can be 'corrected' orally by comparing different versions around the class.

Whilst the dangers of over-reliance on translation have been well-documented, it is important to recognise that using a television sequence as the starting-point does give the activity an 'authentic' dimension which changes its focus from the mechanical manipulation of structure to a device for introducing valid vocabulary reinforcement and developing written accuracy.

★ Note-taking

There are many examples of television programmes which are appropriate as the basis for note-taking practice. Regional news bulletins with some of their short, human interest features, information series on new technological developments and documentaries have proved particularly fertile ground for locating good material. Note-taking is a valid exercise in its own right for developing written skills, but its relevance to the reality of the work-place makes an even stronger case for it to be included in curricula.

An effective strategy is to take a three- or four-minute sequence and to show it through once for orientation and gist comprehension. During a second play-back, pause the tape occasionally at appropriate points to allow learners time to write, before showing the sequence a third time for reinforcement and confirmation. Then allow about fifteen minutes for learners to get their ideas into shape and to re-write their notes in a legible and structured format.

The Channel Tunnel
(*Notes on a four minute feature*)

The Tunnel
- cost £2.3 billion
- 30-minute roll-on, roll-off rail journey
- 30 miles long, 130 feet deep
- train every three minutes
- £49 car plus two adults
- Anglo-French construction

Pro	Con
- speed	- other ports in the South threatened
- convenience	- some unemployment
- creates 30,000 jobs	- breakdown inevitable
- bring Britain and Continent closer	- spread terrorism
	- spread rabies
	- threat to the local environment, etc

In marking note-taking and thus shaping its format, it is probably a good idea to give three marks: one for correctness of language, a second for accuracy of information and a third for the lay-out. This final mark is important since it encourages learners to ask themselves the question *Could I understand these notes in a year's time?* It also stresses the necessity of considering presentation alongside content as a crucial factor in effective written (or printed) communication.

When the activity is first introduced it is better to work on an agreed set of notes with the whole class, so that learners have a clear model of what is expected of them. It can also be helpful before cutting them loose to work by themselves, to provide a few key words and phrases which learners can work into their draft.

★ Summaries

The same strategy can be employed to obtain a summary of a programme or a sequence. The period following the third play-back is then used to produce a piece of succinct and coherent prose. Again, particularly on the first few occasions, it is a good idea to provide learners with plenty of back-up help in the form of keywords and, perhaps, a model summary. This type of activity is quite demanding and it is important to break learners in gently if they are not to feel threatened by it and if they are to 'enjoy' doing it. Experience has shown that where this is done, motivation and commitment are considerably enhanced by working from television rather than text.

★ Report writing

Report writing is a further variation of the same theme, but the source material is likely to be rather longer (ten to fifteen minutes at least) to enable a different technique for introducing it to learners.

Summary work is essentially a 'closed' activity in which there are rights and wrongs and where the learners are asked to record as accurately as possible what was said. They are not expected to express any personal opinion. The writing of a report, on the other hand, can incorporate more scope for individual inventiveness and can enable the same material to be approached from different angles. It is also possible to base the activity on a wide range of programme types.

An effective and enjoyable way of stimulating report writing is to select a programme such as *Yes Minister*. The class is then divided into groups and each group is given a different task. One group might be asked to consider the character of Sir Humphrey, another to comment on political satire, a third to describe the plot, a fourth the humour, and so on.

Given that the initial input may be as long as thirty minutes, it is likely that the group will have to work from one showing, constructing the report from memory, though it may still be advisable to pause the tape occasionally to allow the group to confer and to write down a few key points as they go along. At the end of the programme, the groups are then given time to prepare their report which is likely to be about two hundred words long. They should be encouraged to include a few illustrative examples to make their task easier and to make the final report more interesting.

When the reports are ready, they can be collected in and monitored, or they can be used as the basis for oral work with a member of each group reading out their agreed version to the rest of the class as a precursor to discussion. Obviously, the activity, whilst valuable, is likely to be most appropriate with advanced learners, since it presumes a high level of aural acuity, an ability to discuss themes, plus accurate written work.

★ Script composition

After working for a time on managed tasks and having become familiar with the various media genres, learners are ready to spread their wings and to compose their own scripts. Advertisements and news bulletins are good starting-points as a focus for small-group work. Whilst demanding many of the same skills as traditional essay work, television provides an added motivational boost and makes learners that bit more interested in what they are doing.

As well as composing scripts, the allied activity of writing a commentary is useful. Voice-over documentaries with strong visuals are the best source material. The mechanics of this are rather complex, particularly with large classes, but provided the excerpt can be broken up into sequences of 20 to 30 seconds, which are re-played two or three times, it can be effective.

★ Worksheets

Some of the ideas already outlined in chapters two and three and suggested primarily for the development of listening and speaking skills can readily be adapted to provide written practice in L2. Synonyms, question and answers, keyword contexts, descriptions, gap-fill, stop-frame description, speculation and listening grids are obvious candidates for adaptation.

Much of the development of written skills is likely to be based on worksheets of one sort or another. Simulation tasks such as form-filling, completion of questionnaires and writing applications are familiar, and of particular value are standard worksheets which can be used over and over again with different material. An example of these is the standard worksheet for news bulletins on page 17.

Another is a standard worksheet for advertisements, which offer attractive, punchy, visually effective and easy to handle examplars. The following worksheet provides a framework for ready-made classroom exploitation.

Standard worksheet for advertisements

Brand name? ....

The product or service advertised? ....

....

The target buyer? ....

....

Why? ....

....

Key information about the product? ....

....

Key information about the seller? ....

....

Why should we purchase? ....

....

Examples of 'plus' words (reliable, faster, etc) ....

....

Examples of 'minus' words (dirty, slow, etc) ....

....

Examples of 'action' words (wash, cure, etc) ....

....

How are we being persuaded to buy? ....

....

A good slogan would be: ....

Throughout this chapter the words 'written' or 'writing' have been used. It is, however, increasingly possible to have word processors available to support language teaching and many of the activities described can equally well, and in some cases better, be adapted to the word processor. A later title in this series on micro computers will describe how micros can be used in the classroom and explore in detail some of these suggestions and others.

Reminder

The ideas for the development of listening, speaking and writing skills have been separated partly to stress the importance of introducing listening activities which do not for their outcome demand active oral or written expression. In practice, most of the suggestions in this chapter combine listening with writing, even though the prime focus is on the latter. In a typical lesson it is likely that the teacher would want to merge the three skills and to introduce a number of different activities, so that the effect on the learner is more integrative than might be apparent from the format of this book.

CHAPTER FIVE

Establishing video in the department

★ Video for classroom use

Parkinson's Law can certainly be applied to videos. The more you have, the more you can use. The more you use video, the more proficient and competent you become. There is little doubt that the optimum to aim for is one video station per classroom. Many teachers, when explaining why they don't use video, complain about inaccessability of the one school or departmental machine; the hassle in booking it and the hassle of either moving classes to the video room or the video to the classroom often proves too much. In the hectic life of any institution these are very real obstacles indeed to the effective use of video. If this optimum seems like a fanciful utopia, a unit with monitor and video mounted on a light trolley can provide a short-term solution, but there is no really acceptable alternative to equipping each room with its own system.

Some schools have opted for a video distribution system based on a TV set in each room with a re-play from a centrally located video player in the technician's room. Experience has shown that this does not work well and it is not to be recommended. For any dynamic or creative use of video, it is essential that the teacher has immediate control. Also extremely difficult to organise efficiently is the creation of a departmental video viewing area with groups moving from their classroom to the video room just for the viewing session. Again, if video is to be an integrated part of the language teacher's armoury to be used flexibly and appropriately, it is virtually impossible to introduce efficiently if it has to be booked weeks or even days in advance.

★ Purchasing a video

When purchasing a video, the following questions need to be decided: *Which video recorder? Which system? Which standard?*

WHICH VIDEO RECORDER?

The range of video recorders and players is constantly increasing and changing. There are a number of points to bear in mind, some of them applicable to the general school use of video recorders, others specific to language teaching and learning needs.

● Beware of gimmicks; the more complex (and expensive) machines are, the more likely they are to break down. Simple is often best.

● Go for rugged reliability rather than the latest in casing design or extra facilities.

● Make sure your videos are compatible, not just from the point of view of standards (see below), but of cables. There is nothing more frustrating then to have five videos, with five different types of connector.

- There are basically two ways of distributing a signal: 'R.F' or 'video'. The 'video' method is probably preferable - it is a more solid reliable signal and usually has separate vision and sound distribution cables which enable the introduction of some interesting sound-down and sound-only activities. R.F is the name given to the distribution system to be found in domestic television sets and the connection is made with a single cable of the type that runs from the aerial into the TV set at home. Although both TV receiver and video players are a bit cheaper when the R.F distribution system is used, the signal is not so stable and the quality can be inconsistent. Another advantage of using players and monitors equipped with 'video' signal connections is that when you press 'stop' you don't get a sudden burst of interference noise because the volume is turned up [which is usually the case with 'R.F'].

- Language teachers need to use the still-frame facility more than most other disciplines, so it is important that the video player has one which locks solid, which does not harm the tape and which gives a clean image free of 'picture noise'.

- Similarly, the shuttle-search facility is crucial for locating the right spot for activities which involve a lot of manipulation by the teacher. Shuttle search enables you to see the picture as it winds forward or back and it is preferable to relying on the standard rewind and fast-forward controls where the screen goes blank and you only have the counter for reference. (Always re-wind the tape and set the counter at zero at the beginning of a session thus enabling you to note down the position of key sequences for future reference).

- If you are expecting to record programmes off-air, choose a video that has a simple way of setting the timer. (Some are very complicated and it is easy to make frustrating programming errors.)

- It is worth considering whether or not you are likely to want to edit tapes or to dub (copy) from one tape to another. If so, it is preferable to have videos with both 'R.F' and 'video' connections to allow flexibility of monitoring the signal during editing. Whilst it is possible to edit direct from one machine to another, the quality of the dubbed tape is sometimes unacceptable. Simple and relatively inexpensive editing desks/mixers are increasingly available which considerably reduce the time taken for editing and enhance the quality. The video recorders involved can, of course, still be used for off-air recording and play-back in class.

- Videos will go wrong and it is usually beyond the expertise of most school or departmental technicians to repair them. For this reason it is wise to build into the cost estimates a margin either for a service contract or a sum to enable occasional repairs to be made by outside experts.

N.B. The TV monitor or Receiver is equally important and a few thoughts on their optimum use were set down in Chapter 1.

WHICH SYSTEM?

There are basically four video systems now in contention: **VHS, Betamax, U-Matic** and **Sony-8**.

VHS is the most widely used system in Britain for domestic television in schools. It is, therefore, easier to exchange tapes with other institutions and to use tapes in class which have been recorded at home.

Betamax is similar to VHS in quality, but it is not widely established in Britain. It is really only worth purchasing either if there is no chance of needing compatability with other users in the UK, or if you wish to exchange tapes with users in some countries abroad (e.g. in South and Central America) where Betamax predominates.

U-Matic is more costly than either VHS or Betamax and uses 3/4" tape rather than 1/2" tape as with VHS or Betamax. Also, many of the players on the market are cumbersome when it comes to operating shuttle search or pause facilities. The quality of the recording is, however, usually better and U-matic is particularly useful where you are making master tapes for subsequent dubbing onto VHS or another standard.

Sony-8 is a relatively new system which uses cassettes about the size of an ordinary audio cassette. It is not widely established and therefore prospective purchasers would have to carefully consider the question of compatability with other users' systems. However, the quality is good and because of its size it is particularly appropriate for situations where large numbers of tapes are to be stored - as, for instance, in a media-access centre. There is an added advantage with Sony-8 in that since it is not widely used on the domestic market the cassettes are rarely stolen (definitely not the case with VHS).

WHICH STANDARD?

Worldwide there are three basic broadcasting standards in operation for terrestrial distribution with a further two standards emerging for satellite transmissions. In the UK and most of Europe the signal distributed by the broadcasting stations is called PAL. In France, Russia and most francophone countries, the standard used is called SECAM. In North, Central and South America the broadcasting standard is called NTSC. What this means in practice is that if you are recording off-air or playing back tapes the video recorder must be a PAL standard recorder for PAL signals, a SECAM standard recorder for SECAM signals and an NTSC standard recorder for NTSC originated material. If you try to play on a PAL player in Britain a tape recorded in America you will not get a picture. If you try to play a SECAM tape on a PAL system you will get the signal, but only in black and white.

It is possible to purchase triple standard video recorders but they must be linked to triple standard monitors in order to display the signal. Although they work perfectly well they are considerably more expensive. It is worth noting that if you wish to record and play back authentic French television a cheaper solution might be to set up a satellite recording system since the French broadcast their TV 5 satellite programmes using the PAL standard.

★ Making off-air recordings

The usual pattern for organising recordings seems to be that initially the person within a department who has taken the initiative in introducing video is landed with the task of arranging the off-air recordings. As use builds up and other colleagues become interested, it clearly makes sense to centralise requests for, and the organisation of recordings. This can be allocated to a member of the academic staff, to a technician or to the library. There are clearly too many permutations of need, of size of institution, of internal structures to attempt to outline any prescriptive formula for this, but it is worth bearing in mind the following points to support the efficient operation of a system.

- Ensure that enough money is allocated to enable the purchase of sufficient video tapes to meet demand over a year.

- Considerable discounts exist for bulk purchases of tapes.

- In general, for 'heavy' classroom use, 120 minute tapes are preferable to 180 as they are usually thicker and more robust.

- On every tape cassette there is a small 'window' covered usually by a piece of plastic. Whilst the plastic is in place the tape can be used for both recording or playback. If it is removed the cassette cannot subsequently be used for recording unless the 'window' is covered up in some way. It is a good idea to remove the plastic on tapes that you are likely to use on multiple occasions over a period of time to prevent accidental erasure.

- All cassettes should be clearly labelled with the series, the programme and the running time.

- Periodic lists of tapes held 'on the shelf' or in the library should be issued partly to remind colleagues of what exists, to encourage use and to avoid duplication, and partly to enable the re-cycling of tapes no longer needed.

- As the use of video grows, it is essential to have coordination at departmental level. This enables discussion of aims and objectives and the exchange of information. It also provides information for appropriate purchasing decisions to be made. Many institutions operate a simple 'report' system with a form attached to the cassette cover for teachers to note any good or bad features of the programme material.

- Although many courses come complete with teacher's and student's notes, there is often a need for the production of 'in-house' ancilliary material. Since this is obviously time-consuming, it is again best coordinated at departmental level with colleagues producing worksheets, etc according to an agreed brief and then making the material available to a departmental pool. (The availability of support materials should also be noted on the 'report form' attached to the cover).

- If a central recording system is used the classroom video recorders can be 'play-back' only. These work out cheaper than videos with timer and record facilities.

- Where there is heavy use made of a recording system, it is essential to have back-up equipment. If, for instance, a department has purchased 'play-back' only machines for classroom use, at least two machines should be available for making recordings.

★ Self-access video

Institutions are increasingly wanting to make video available to students on a self-access basis. There are several reasons for this:

- students can work at their own pace, thus getting more out of the material than when they have no individual control;

- they can pursue their own special interests outside the tightly controlled framework of a taught course;

- they are motivated to spend more time on language learning than when the only 'input' is the classroom lesson;

- it is possible to develop innovative learning patterns with periods of self-access study complementing the more formal instruction sessions. It gives concrete form to student-centred learning;

- a self-access centre can provide an excellent environment for supporting project work;

- opportunities can be easily provided for remedial work, for extra reinforcement or for enabling students to catch up if they have missed a session.

Whilst these advantages are real, there are relatively few examples of self-access centres that work well. Financial constraints are clearly a major factor, from the point of view both of equipment and staff-time. Some administrators have embraced self-access/autonomous learning as a way of saving on staff, but in reality the converse is true - such centres generate more work rather than less. Students are indeed often enthusiastic about self-access, but experience has shown that they need clear guidance on how to learn and how to manage the resources efficiently.

My own view is that it is well worth-while establishing self-learn language facilities to enhance the learning experience, but that a great deal of careful thought needs to go into the planning and execution if they are to be effective.

There is too wide a range of constraints and priorities to attempt to describe an ideal model centre. On the one hand, it may be that it is appropriate to do little more than to have one or two videos in the library; on the other, a large institution might be able to establish a learning centre with numerous machines, backed up by resources, staff and by a commitment to develop Action Learning for all its courses which revolve around the self-learn facilities.

Since the establishment of a self-access centre must inevitably be the result of team work and group discussion, here are a few key questions to debate and resolve.

- Is video to be part of a comprehensive resource centre involving perhaps sound replay facilities and computers?

- What role could a self-access video facility have in relation to the overall teaching and learning within the institution? Is it to have the status of an optional extra; is it to be used for occasional integrated work such as projects; are there opportunities for radically re-shaping the whole teaching/learning patterns within the institution?

- How should the introduction be organised? In phased stages from a modest beginning (probably preferable) or a 'big bang' approach?

- What equipment will be purchased and have all the details for a specification been considered? (For instance, the TV monitor should have a socket to enable earphones to be connected with sufficient power and quality to accommodate at least two sets of head-phones).

- Where will it be located and what will the configuration be?

- What furniture is needed and decorations? Experience suggests that the more informal, the more colourful, the more lively the atmosphere, the more it will be used. The overall impression should be closer to a 'supermarket' than a quiet closed-access library.

- Have all the costs been considered? The equipment, the furnishings, the decoration, the soft-ware, technical support, staff time for training, developing materials, organising and administration?

- Who will be responsible for coordination and organisation? It is important not to underestimate the time this will take, particularly as a lot of counselling will be necessary at least initially.

- How can an efficient system be evolved for cataloguing, labelling and displaying the soft-ware?

- Is it feasible to include ancilliary materials such as worksheets and transcripts? This is obviously ideal but again involves a considerable time commitment.

- How can students (and staff) be kept informed of what is on offer and encouraged to make optimum use of the facilities?

- What arrangements are viable to monitor the success of the facilities in general and individual programmes in particular?

- How can the need for constantly updating and extending the soft-ware and ancillary materials be accommodated?

This list of matters to discuss may seem a little formidable at first sight, particularly for modest facilities. However, any of the questions can be answered fairly rapidly. There is no doubt that the thrust towards student-centred learning is now firmly established and that self-access centres are likely to prove crucial in making such initiatives viable and effective. It is, therefore, worth grasping the nettle and attempting to start the ball rolling.

GLOSSARY

Included in this section are some useful definitions to help when discussing video with salespeople or technicians, a list of addresses, and some suggestions for further reading.

Definitions

Amplifier: a piece of equipment which you connect to the 'sound out' socket on the video player and which improves the quality of the sound significantly. Linked to a large loudspeaker for classroom use, it enables precise control of bass and treble and produces a clearer, crisper, more comprehensible signal.

Betamax: the name given to a type of video player which once rivalled VHS-standard players but which is not now common in Britain, though it is still found in other countries notably in South America.

B.N.C Connector: a bayonet-type plug/socket connector which is most commonly used when the signal is being distributed at 'video' frequency (not R.F - see 'video' below).

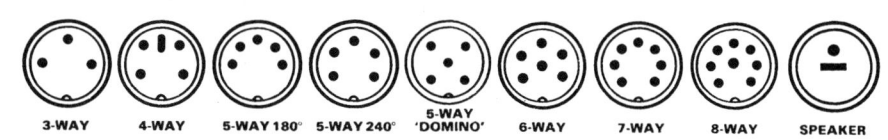

BNC straight plug

BNC straight jack

'DIN' style audio connectors

3-WAY   4-WAY   5-WAY 180°   5-WAY 240°   5-WAY 'DOMINO'   6-WAY   7-WAY   8-WAY   SPEAKER

These connectors have silver-plated pins and sockets and are rated at 100 V a.c./150 V d.c. at 2 A.

screened range
cable mounting

L.59
Dia.15

Dub:　　　　　　　the process by which you copy the video programme (or soundtrack) from one tape to another.

D-Mac:　　　　　　the name given for the distribution signal standard from some of the new satellite channels (as opposed to PAL or SECAM, see below). To receive D-Mac signals you can still use a standard domestic TV receiver, but only when used in conjunction with a 'black-box' to encode the signal into PAL (or SECAM).

Edit:　　　　　　　the process of selecting/shortening programme material by transferring parts of a video programme from one tape to another. It can be done simply by linking two videos together with their 'output'/'input' sockets, but better results are obtained if a video editor is used enabling you to be more accurate, to obtain cleaner cuts and a higher quality picture.

Euroconnector:　　a multi-pin type of connector most frequently found in micro-computers, but used occasionally on some video monitors.

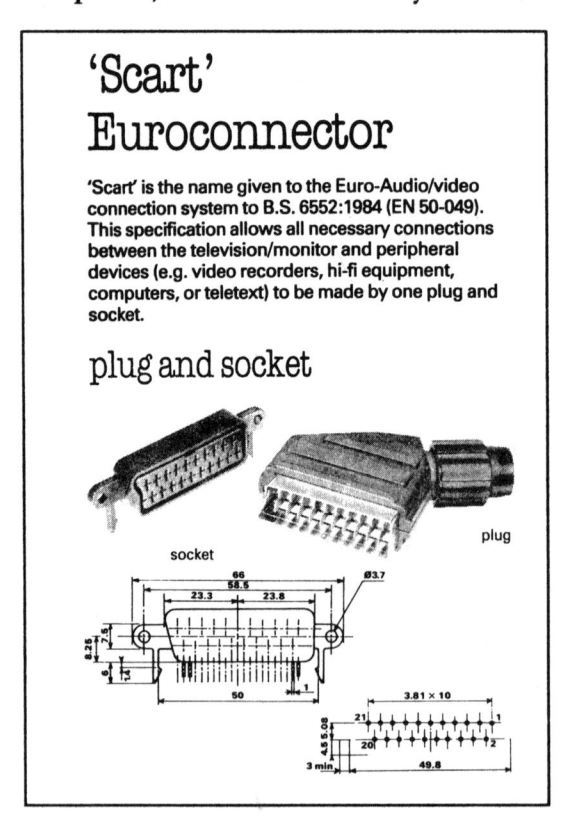

'Scart' Euroconnector

'Scart' is the name given to the Euro-Audio/video connection system to B.S. 6552:1984 (EN 50-049). This specification allows all necessary connections between the television/monitor and peripheral devices (e.g. video recorders, hi-fi equipment, computers, or teletext) to be made by one plug and socket.

plug and socket

Freeze-frame:　　obtained when you press 'pause'. It is a particularly useful facility in language teaching. When purchasing a new video it is worth getting one which produces a 'clean' picture, i.e. a solid picture without 'noise bars' across it. With certain models of video players there is a slight delay in hearing the sound-track when the 'pause' is released. This can prove aggravating in some of the activities suggested in the previous chapters, so it is worth checking before purchase that the sound comes back immediately the 'pause' is released.

Jackplug: 'push-in' connectors which come in various sizes and are used primarily with head-phones.

0·25 in commercial

Commercial grade connectors for general purpose applications.

2-pole

insulated plug

screened plug

insulated line socket

S.S.M. = 10

Loud-speaker: the instrument by which the sound is delivered to viewers. The internal loud-speakers on TV sets are often very small and only really suitable for use in a small room at home. It is preferable for classroom work to have a larger external loud-speaker, preferably though not necessarily used in conjunction with an external amplifier. The use of an external loud-speaker can dramatically improve the quality and audibility of a sound-track.

Monitor: the name given for a TV set which operates at 'video' frequency, i.e. it will not take the ordinary R.F signal used in domestic TV receivers.

Noise: in addition to 'sound noise', video replays can be affected by 'picture noise' - usually patterns of interference across the screen. The most common causes of picture noise are 'tracking' faults and dirty play-back/record heads on the video. The former can normally be overcome by adjusting the tracking control knob on the video player. Dirty heads can be cleaned in a few seconds using a cleaning cassette. This is obtainable from most video suppliers and just inserted in the video in the normal way. It is advisable to clean the heads regularly, particularly if you are using old tapes where the oxide coating is beginning to flake off.

NTSC:	the broadcast signal standard used primarily in North and South America. To play back tapes recorded on the NTSC standard you need a triple standard video player and associated triple standard TV receiver.
PAL:	the broadcast signal standard used in Britain and most of Europe. It is, therefore, usually possible to exchange tapes with institutions in, for instance, Germany.
Receiver:	a television set which receives the signal using the standard domestic 'R.F' frequency (as opposed to a 'monitor' which uses the 'video' frequency).
R.F:	stands for 'Radio Frequency' and it is the frequency at which broadcasts are received in ordinary domestic TV sets. Although it is perfectly possible to link video players and TV sets using the standard R.F domestic aerial type connector, it is often preferable to use the alternative 'video' distribution frequency. (See 'video' below.)
Secam:	the broadcast signal standard used in France, in most francophone countries and in Russia. A tape recorded on a 'SECAM' video recorder will play back on a 'PAL' system, but only in black and white. To obtain a colour re-play you need a triple-standard player and associated triple-standard TV set.
Shuttle-search:	an important facility to be found on most modern video recorders. This enables the tape to be wound forwards or backwards at speed with a fast-moving picture flashing across the screen. It facilitates the precise and rapid location of sequences to be used in the classroom. (When the 're-wind' or 'fast-forward' control is selected the tape winds much faster and the screen goes blank.)
Slow-motion:	not a vital facility in the classroom but it can be used to effect in activities such as 'commentary' work where you need more time to think of what to say. When the slow motion control is used the picture slows down and the sound cuts off.
Sony-8:	a new type of video system which produces a good quality signal and uses video cassettes roughly the size of ordinary sound cassettes. It is not widely found but it is particularly appropriate when large numbers of programmes are being stored in libraries or self-access centres.
Tracking:	a control to be found on most video recorders to ensure a good quality replay of tapes recorded on other machines. It is not frequently needed as most recorders are now synchronised to the same recording standard, but adjusting the tracking control is sometimes necessary to clean up a 'wobbly' or 'noisy' picture.

Tuner: the part of the television receiver which enables you to tune in to different frequencies and thus obtain different channels. Once a channel has been tuned in you do not normally have to touch it, but sometimes bad colour, buzz on the sound-track or lines across the screen can be eliminated by a fine tuning adjustment. Incidentally, this only applies when you are using the 'R.F' system of signal distribution and not when you have connected the monitor and player using the 'video' frequency connection.

U-matic: an alternative video system to VHS and Betamax. It uses 3/4" tape and produces a slightly better quality of picture. Primarily found in semi-professional recording facilities, it is more expensive than the alternatives and not, therefore, advisable for normal classroom use.

VHS: the most common type of video system to be found in Britain. VHS dominates the domestic market and although the reproduction quality is no better than with Betamax, U-matic or Sony-8, compatability with other institutions and with home recorders makes it the most frequently selected system.

Video: the name given to the recorder/player but also to the distribution signal frequency used as an alternative to the familiar domestic 'R.F' connection. The 'video' frequency signal is usually cleaner and more solid than the 'R.F' signal, it does not need adjusting and you do not get a burst of sound interference when you press the 'stop' control on the video recorder. (An aggravating feature of most 'R.F' distribution systems.)

Some useful addresses for information on videos and TV programmes

BBC
Educational Broadcasting Information, BBC, London W12 0TT
BBC Enterprises, Woodlands, 80 Wood Lane, London W12 0TT
BBC English by Radio & Television, Bush House, PO Box 76, London WC2B 4PH

Brighton Polytechnic
The Language Centre, Falmer, Brighton BN1 9PH

British Council
Media Department, 10 Spring Gardens, London SW1A 2BN

CILT
Regent's College, Inner Circle, Regent's Park, London NW1 4NS

Goethe-Institut
50 Princes Gate, Exhibition Road, London SW7 2PH

Institut Français
17 Queensbury Place, London SW7 2DT

Italian Institute
39 Belgrave Square, London SW1X 8NX

Longman
Longman House, Burnt Hill, Harlow, Essex

Macmillan Education
Brunel Road, Houndmill Industrial Estate, Basingstoke, Hants. RG21 2XS

Mary Glasgow Publications
Avenue House, 131-133 Holland Park Avenue, London W11 4UT

Nelson Filmscan
Nelson House, Mayfield Road, Walton on Thames, Surrey KT12 5PL

Open University
Milton Keynes, Bedfordshire

Pitman Publishing
128 Long Acre, London WC2E 9AN

Spanish Institute
102 Eaton Square, London SW1W 9AN

Thames Television
149 Tottenham Court Road, London W1P 9LL

Ideas for further reading

Allan, M (1985) *Teaching English with video*, Longman

Bates, A W (1984) *Broadcasting in education*, Constable

Geddes, M (1981) *Communication in the classroom*, Edited by Johnson, K & Morrow, K.

Geddes, M (1982) *Video in the language classroom*, Modern English Publications

Hill, B (1982) *Learning alone, some implications for course design in 'individualisation'*, Modern English Publications

Lonergan, J (1984) *Video in language teaching*, Cambridge University Press

Tomalin, B (1986) *Video, TV & radio in the English class*, Macmillan